Medical Terminology Prefixes Quiz

Alexander McRose

Disclaimer and Terms of Use

Dedication

To R.I. who motivates and comforts me.

Introduction

You know that medical terminology can be quite tricky, and that the Latinate prefixes may have several different meanings, or that they may seem similar, while, in fact, they refer to completely different concepts. This proves to be a challenge for anyone who aims to become an expert in the medical field.

Are you certain that you know everything about medical terminology prefixes?

Are you ready to prove this?

The medical terminology prefixes quiz will test your current knowledge of this subject. The point of this quiz is to give you some idea where you stand and what areas you need to focus on to pass the real exam.

Medical Terminology Prefixes Quiz Book with 240 questions and answers is a must-have for medical students, postgraduates, practitioners, nurses, medical assistants, and healthcare professionals all over the world!

Are you ready to start?

Good luck!

Quiz Instructions

1. The book contains 4 chapters with 60 questons each. Each of the 4 chapters is divided into four rounds of fifteen questions.

2. We recommend that you download, open, and print out the answer form, which is to be found at the end of the book. This will make the whole procedure much easier, as you won't have to write down the answers in separate columns on your own.

3. For each multiple choice question, you should read the question and circle the correct answer in the answer form.

4. After each round of questions, the correct answers are provided. You can choose whether you would like to see the correct answers immediately after having completed the round, or you can do the whole test and check all the 240 answers.

Table of Contents

CHAPTER 1 - What Does the Prefix Refer To?

Chapter 1 - Round 1 Questions

1. The prefix pertaining to blood vessel is:

A. bas(o)-
B. angi(o)-
C. cerebell(o)-
D. cerebr(o)-

2. The prefix pertaining to the armpit is:

A. capit-
B. bucc(o)-
C. axill-
D. lapar(o)-

3. The prefix pertaining to the heart is:

A. neur(o)-
B. onych(o)-
C. cardi(o)-
D. pedo-

4. The prefix pertaining to the wrist is:

A. carp(o)-
B. ren(o)-
C. ca-
D. viscer(o)-

5. The prefix pertaining to eye's pupil is:

A. blephar(o)-
B. co-
C. cyst(o)-
D. coro-

6. The prefix pertaining to the intestine is:

A. dacry(o)-
B. enter(o)-
C. faci(o)-
D. ent-

7. The prefix pertaining to the gums is:

A. gin-
B. ischio-
C. gingiv-
D. nas(o)-

8. The prefix pertaining to the shoulder is:

A. humer(o)-
B. pleur(o)-
C. hamer(o)-
D. ren(o)-

9. The prefix pertaining to the nipple is:

A. nippl(o)-
B. uter(o)-
C. vesic(o)-
D. mammill(o)-

10. The prefix pertaining to the kidney is:

A. viscer(o)-
B. nephr(o)-
C. axill-
D. neg-

11. The prefix pertaining to the lungs is:

A. pnom(o)-
B. pneum(o)-
C. lung(o)-
D. episi(o)-

12. The prefix pertaining to the neck is:

A. trachel(o)-
B. carp(o)-
C. amni-
D. ab-

13. The prefix pertaining to an artery is:

A. arrte(o)-
B. art-
C. cost(o)-
D. arteri(o)-

14. The prefix pertaining to joints is:

A. onych(o)-
B. arthr(o)-
C. ar(o)-
D. nas(o)-

15. The prefix pertaining to hair is:

A. alope(o)-
B. peo-
C. capill-
D. ventr(o)-

Chapter 1 - Round 1 Correct Answer Sheet

1. B

2. C

3. C

4. A

5. D

6. B

7. C

8. A

9. D

10. B

11. B

12. A

13. D

14. B

15. C

Chapter 1 - Round 2 Questions

16. The prefix pertaining to gallbladder is:

A. cholecyst(o)-
B. chol(o)-
C. aur(i)-
D. glott(o)-

17. The prefix pertaining to teeth is:

A. mast(o)-
B. dent-
C. de-
D. or(o)-

18. The prefix pertaining to the pubic region is:

A. ot(o)-
B. ep-
C. episi(o)-
D. salping(o)-

19. The prefix pertaining to the jaw is:

A. gnath(o)-
B. trachel(o)-
C. gna-
D. viscer(o)-

20. The prefix pertaining to the lip is:

A. la-
B. lipi(o)-
C. lip-
D. labi(o)-

21. The prefix pertaining to the hand is:

A. bas(o)-
B. manu-
C. cerebell(o)-
D. ma-

22. The prefix pertaining to the woman's is:

A. humer(o)-
B. hymer(o)-
C. oophor(o)-
D. oomer(o)-

23. The prefix pertaining to the penis is:

A. peo-
B. penis-
C. peni(o)-
D. gnath(o)-

24. The prefix pertaining to blood is:

A. trachel(o)-
B. bacteri(o)-
C. sanguine-
D. bucc(o)-

25. The prefix pertaining to the ear is:

A. aurae(o)-
B. eur(o)-
C. aur(i)-
D. eura(i)-

26. The prefix pertaining to anus is:

A. ann-
B. anus(o)-
C. aanus-
D. an-

27. The prefix pertaining to the neck is:

A. cervic-
B. capill-
C. carpic-
D. genu-

28. The prefix pertaining to the ribs is:

A. coss(o)-
B. cyst(o)-
C. co-
D. cost(o)-

29. The prefix pertaining to the forehead is:

A. fr(o)-
B. front-
C. fraea-
D. fore(o)-

30. The prefix pertaining to the tongue is:

A. lingu(o)-
B. tongu(o)-
C. lin-
D. tong-

Chapter 1 - Round 2 Correct Answer Sheet

16. A

17. B

18. C

19. A

20. D

21. B

22. C

23. A

24. C

25. C

26. D

27. A

28. D

29. B

30. A

Chapter 1 - Round 3 Questions

31. The prefix pertaining to base is:

A. ba-
B. bas(o)-
C. blephar(o)-
D. capit-

32. The prefix pertaining to the cheek is:

A. ischio-
B. faci(o)-
C. bucc(o)-
D. nas(o)-

33. The prefix pertaining to the back is:

A. dors(o)-
B. derm(o)-
C. episi(o)-
D. or(o)-

34. The prefix pertaining to the liver is:

A. humer(o)-
B. hepat-
C. hyster(o)-
D. he-

35. The prefix pertaining to the nose is:

A. capill-
B. axill-
C. capit-
D. nas(o)-

36. The prefix pertaining to the nervous system is:

A. syst(o)-
B. ner-
C. enter(o)-
D. neur(o)-

37. The prefix pertaining to bacteria is:

A. ba-
B. bac(o)-
C. bacteri(o)-
D. capit-

38. The prefix pertaining to the hand is:

A. chur(o)-
B. chi-
C. gingiv-
D. chir(o)-

39. The prefix pertaining to tears is:

A. pleur(o)-
B. labi(o)-
C. dacry(o)-
D. vesic(o)-

40. The prefix pertaining to the knee is:

A. genu-
B. zenu-
C. benu-
D. fenu-

41. The prefix pertaining to the womb is:

A. humer(o)-
B. hyster(o)-
C. glott(o)-
D. glatt(o)-

42. The prefix pertaining to the breast is:

A. ma-
B. mast(o)-
C. bast(o)-
D. ba-

43. The prefix pertaining to the ear is:

A. ot(o)-
B. et(o)-
C. ge(o)-
D. be(o)-

44. The prefix pertaining to the mind is:

A. ps-
B. dacry(o)-
C. psych(o)-
D. dac-

45. The prefix pertaining to the spine is:

A. spi(o)-
B. spondyl(o)-
C. spon(o)-
D. span(o)-

Chapter 1 - Round 3 Correct Answer Sheet

31. B

32. C

33. A

34. B

35. D

36. D

37. C

38. D

39. C

40. A

41. B

42. B

43. A

44. C

45. B

Chapter 1 - Round 4 Questions

46. The prefix pertaining to the belly is:

A. ve-
B. ver(o)-
C. intr(o)-
D. ventr(o)-

47. The prefix pertaining to the eyelid is:

A. episi(o)-
B. faci(o)-
C. blephar(o)-
D. gingiv-

48. The prefix pertaining to the brain is:

A. cerebr(o)-
B. cer-
C. psych(o)-
D. psy-

49. The prefix pertaining to bile is:

A. bil(o)-
B. chol(e)-
C. bi-
D. nas(o)-

50. The prefix pertaining to urinary bladder is:

A. hyster(o)-
B. ischio-
C. cerebr(o)-
D. cyst(o)-

51. The prefix pertaining to the stomach is:

A. gastr(o)-
B. uter(o)-
C. ventr(o)-
D. viscer(o)-

52. The prefix pertaining to the tongue is:

A. lingu(o)-
B. tongu(o)-
C. gloss(o)-
D. nas(o)-

53. The prefix pertaining to the abdomen-wall is:

A. lapa-
B. lapar(o)-
C. la-
D. abd(o)-

54. The prefix pertaining to the eye is:

A. ot(o)-
B. oophor(o)-
C. onych(o)-
D. ocul(o)-

55. The prefix pertaining to the child is:

A. pedo-
B. chir(o)-
C. chol(e)-
D. bucc(o)-

56. The prefix pertaining to the ribs is:

A. colp(o)-
B. gloss(o)-
C. pleur(o)-
D. labi(o)-

57. The prefix pertaining to the kidney is:

A. run(o)-
B. ren(o)-
C. ran(o)-
D. ryn(o)-

58. The prefix pertaining to the navel is:

A. umic-
B. umbic-
C. bilic-
D. umbilic-

59. The prefix pertaining to the bladder is:

A. vesic(o)-
B. resic(o)-
C. desic(o)-
D. pesic(o)-

60. The prefix pertaining to the internal organs is:

A. discer(o)-
B. ciscer(o)-
C. miscer(o)-
D. viscer(o)-

Chapter 1 - Round 4 Correct Answer Sheet

46. D

47. C

48. A

49. B

50. D

51. A

52. C

53. B

54. D

55. A

56. C

57. B

58. D

59. A

60. D

CHAPTER 2 - Meaning of the Prefix

Chapter 2 - Round 1 Questions

1. The prefix meaning through is:

A. bia-
B. dia-
C. fia-
D. dya-

2. The prefix meaning spindle is:

A. plostr-
B. flostr-
C. clostr-
D. clystr-

3. The prefix meaning separation is:

A. fis-
B. nis-
C. dis-
D. pis-

4. The prefix meaning before is:

A. fore-
B. core-
C. dore-
D. more-

5. The prefix meaning below is:

A. in-
B. inf-
C. intra-
D. infra-

6. The prefix meaning same is:

A. ipsy-
B. ipsi-
C. epsi-
D. opsi-

7. The prefix meaning part is:

A. fero-
B. gero-
C. mero-
D. nero-

8. The prefix meaning bone is:

A. ossi-
B. essi-
C. assi-
D. ussi-

9. The prefix meaning few is:

A. nauci-
B. fauci
C. mauci-
D. pauci-

10. The prefix meaning after is:

A. cost-
B. post-
C. rost-
D. dost-

11. The prefix meaning muscular is:

A. marco-
B. sarco-
C. narco-
D. darco-

12. The prefix meaning slow is:

A. brady-
B. frady-
C. grady-
D. br-

13. The prefix meaning together is:

A. nom-
B. fom-
C. dom-
D. com-

14. The prefix meaning sweet is:

A. fluco-
B. gluco-
C. pluco-
D. glu-

15. The prefix meaning upon is:

A. opi-
B. api-
C. epi-
D. upi-

Chapter 2 - Round 1 Correct Answer Sheet

1. B

2. C

3. C

4. A

5. D

6. B

7. C

8. A

9. D

10. B

11. B

12. A

13. D

14. B

15. C

Chapter 2 - Round 2 Questions

16. The prefix meaning against is:

A. anti-
B. an-
C. enti-
D. semi-

17. The prefix meaning down is:

A. data-
B. cata-
C. mata-
D. fata-

18. The prefix meaning away is:

A. ic-
B. oc-
C. ec-
D. ac-

19. The prefix meaning one-half is:

A. hemi-
B. femi-
C. nemi-
D. bemi-

20. The prefix meaning within is:

A. ontra-
B. antra-
C. entra-
D. intra-

21. The prefix meaning lateral is:

A. la-
B. latero-
C. lat-
D. lato-

22. The prefix meaning new is:

A. meo-
B. deo-
C. neo-
D. beo-

23. The prefix meaning thick is:

A. pachy-
B. pa-
C. pac-
D. nachy-

24. The prefix meaning to grow is:

A. ph-
B. mhyt-
C. phyt-
D. shyt-

25. The prefix meaning behind is:

A. metro-
B. re-
C. retro-
D. tro-

26. The prefix meaning under is:

A. pub-
B. nub-
C. dub-
D. sub-

27. The prefix meaning emotions is:

A. thym-
B. th-
C. sh-
D. shym-

28. The prefix meaning pressure is:

A. mono-
B. fo-
C. fono-
D. tono-

29. The prefix meaning primitive is:

A. pr-
B. arch-
C. ar-
D. prim-

30. The prefix meaning break is:

A. clast-
B. blast-
C. cl-
D. bl-

Chapter 2 - Round 2 Correct Answer Sheet

16. A

17. B

18. C

19. A

20. D

21. B

22. C

23. A

24. C

25. C

26. D

27. A

28. D

29. B

30. A

Chapter 2 - Round 3 Questions

31. The prefix meaning twice is:

A. ti-
B. bi-
C. di-
D. fi-

32. The prefix meaning abnormal is:

A. dos-
B. dis-
C. dys-
D. cys-

33. The prefix meaning outside is:

A. extra-
B. ex-
C. out-
D. outra-

34. The prefix meaning between is:

A. int-
B. inter-
C. bet-
D. bit-

35. The prefix meaning nucleus is:

A. nuc-
B. nucle-
C. kar-
D. karyo-

36. The prefix meaning thousandth is:

A. mi-
B. th-
C. thou-
D. milli-

37. The prefix meaning normal is:

A. nor-
B. no-
C. normo-
D. vert-

38. The prefix meaning volume is:

A. enco-
B. inco-
C. enci-
D. onco-

39. The prefix meaning small is:

A. pic-
B. par-
C. parvo-
D. pico-

40. The prefix meaning more is:

A. pleio-
B. plaio-
C. pluio-
D. plyio-

41. The prefix meaning itching is:

A. ps-
B. psor-
C. pse-
D. pser-

42. The prefix meaning strength is:

A. sth-
B. stheno-
C. ben-
D. beno-

43. The prefix meaning childbirth is:

A. toco-
B. to-
C. loco-
D. lo-

44. The prefix meaning beyond is:

A. ult-
B. ext-
C. ultra-
D. extra-

45. The prefix meaning from is:

A. aa-
B. ab-
C. ac-
D. ad-

Chapter 2 - Round 3 Correct Answer Sheet

31. B

32. C

33. A

34. B

35. D

36. D

37. C

38. D

39. C

40. A

41. B

42. B

43. A

44. C

45. B

Chapter 2 - Round 4 Questions

46. The prefix meaning after is:

A. me-
B. afte-
C. pre-
D. meta-

47. The prefix meaning abnormal is:

A. pa-
B. abno-
C. para-
D. ab-

48. The prefix meaning before is:

A. pre-
B. be-
C. befo-
D. para-

49. The prefix meaning rigid is:

A. rig-
B. tetan-
C. tet-
D. ri-

50. The prefix meaning three is:

A. thr-
B. th-
C. trico-
D. tri-

51. The prefix meaning again is:

A. ana-
B. aga-
C. aba-
D. ada-

52. The prefix meaning down is:

A. do-
B. di-
C. de-
D. dy-

53. The prefix meaning restriction is:

A. res-
B. isch-
C. is-
D. rest-

54. The prefix meaning ten thousand is:

A. mili-
B. micro-
C. pico-
D. myri-

55. The prefix meaning through is:

A. per-
B. tre-
C. cro-
D. uro-

56. The prefix meaning food is:

A. mito-
B. zito-
C. sito-
D. mi-

57. The prefix meaning lens-shaped is:

A. len-
B. phaco-
C. lenso-
D. le-

58. The prefix meaning extreme is:

A. hyp-
B. ext-
C. extre-
D. hyper-

59. The prefix meaning new is:

A. eu-
B. neu-
C. nuvo-
D. ne-

60. The prefix meaning separated from is:

A. sepa-
B. sep-
C. ap-
D. apo-

Chapter 2 - Round 4 Correct Answer Sheet

46. D

47. C

48. A

49. B

50. D

51. A

52. C

53. B

54. D

55. A

56. C

57. B

58. D

59. A

60. D

CHAPTER 3 - What Does the Prefix Mean?

Chapter 3 - Round 1 Questions

1. The prefix arch- means:

A. abnormal
B. primitive
C. beyond normal
D. muscular

2. The prefix clostr- means:

A. first
B. difficult
C. spindle
D. tense

3. The prefix dif- means:

A. restriction
B. diference
C. separation
D. strength

4. The prefix epi- means:

A. upon
B. anus
C. behind
D. childbirth

5. The prefix fore- means:

A. toward
B. through
C. sweet
D. ahead

6. The prefix infra- means:

A. backward
B. below
C. muscular
D. conduction

7. The prefix micro- means:

A. small
B. big
C. millionth
D. thousandth

8. The prefix ossi- means:

A. bone
B. difficult
C. cycle
D. abnormal

9. The prefix parvo- means:

A. difficult
B. beyond normal
C. sweet
D. small

10. The prefix post- means:

A. one-half
B. after
C. primitive
D. pressure

11. The prefix retro- means:

A. old
B. behind
C. new
D. toward

12. The prefix semi- means:

A. one-half
B. separation
C. difficult
D. outside

13. The prefix super- means:

A. big
B. strength
C. sweet
D. superior

14. The prefix toco- means:

A. through
B. childbirth
C. to grow
D. together

15. The prefix isch- means:

A. itching
B. life
C. restriction
D. muscular

Chapter 3 - Round 1 Correct Answer Sheet

1. B

2. C

3. C

4. A

5. D

6. B

7. C

8. A

9. D

10. B

11. B

12. A

13. D

14. B

15. C

Chapter 3 - Round 2 Questions

16. The prefix ana- means:

A. again
B. anal
C. ahead
D. below

17. The prefix bio- means:

A. from
B. life
C. more
D. outside

18. The prefix de- means:

A. difficult
B. double
C. from
D. slow

19. The prefix dia- means:

A. through
B. difficult
C. double
D. down

20. The prefix eu- means:

A. equal
B. few
C. fast
D. new

21. The prefix hyper- means:

A. below
B. beyond normal
C. restriction
D. separation

22. The prefix meta- means:

A. more
B. muscular
C. beyond
D. one-half

23. The prefix onco- means:

A. volume
B. without
C. new
D. old

24. The prefix pauci- means:

A. sharp
B. strength
C. few
D. through

25. The prefix pre- means:

A. primitive
B. pressure
C. before
D. separated from

26. The prefix stheno- means:

A. sharp
B. slow
C. through
D. strength

27. The prefix thym- means:

A. emotions
B. together
C. toward
D. to grow

28. The prefix trans- means:

A. thick
B. difficult
C. trance
D. through

29. The prefix com- means:

A. more
B. together
C. conduction
D. childbirth

30. The prefix dromo- means:

A. conduction
B. pressure
C. separation
D. thick

Chapter 3 - Round 2 Correct Answer Sheet

16. A

17. B

18. C

19. A

20. D

21. B

22. C

23. A

24. C

25. C

26. D

27. A

28. D

29. B

30. A

Chapter 3 - Round 3 Questions

31. The prefix ad- means:

A. ahead
B. toward
C. again
D. before

32. The prefix bi- means:

A. beyond
B. below
C. double
D. behind

33. The prefix apo- means:

A. separated from
B. abnormal
C. food
D. difficult

34. The prefix cutane- means:

A. conduction
B. skin
C. childbirth
D. more

35. The prefix diplo- means:

A. down
B. double
C. from
D. twofold

36. The prefix hemi- means:

A. millionth
B. fast
C. lateral
D. one-half

37. The prefix neo- means:

A. sharp
B. neon
C. new
D. first

38. The prefix para- means:

A. primitive
B. pressure
C. paralel
D. abnormal

39. The prefix prim- means:

A. primitive
B. sweet
C. first
D. together

40. The prefix scoto- means:

A. darkness
B. skin
C. sharp
D. more

41. The prefix tetan- means:

A. to grow
B. tense
C. together
D. treatment

42. The prefix tono- means:

A. ten thousand
B. pressure
C. thousandth
D. together

43. The prefix dys- means:

A. difficult
B. double
C. emotions
D. first

44. The prefix iso- means:

A. itching
B. on this side
C. equal
D. double

45. The prefix myri- means:

A. thousandth
B. ten thousand
C. millionth
D. fourth

Chapter 3 - Round 3 Correct Answer Sheet

31. B

32. C

33. A

34. B

35. D

36. D

37. C

38. D

39. C

40. A

41. B

42. B

43. A

44. C

45. B

Chapter 3 - Round 4 Questions

46. The prefix ab- means:

A. abnormal
B. abdomen
C. behind
D. away from

47. The prefix brady- means:

A. beyond normal
B. conduction
C. slow
D. fast

48. The prefix cis- means:

A. on this side
B. on both side
C. invisible
D. strong

49. The prefix ec- means:

A. emotions
B. away
C. equal
D. more

50. The prefix gluco- means:

A. below
B. outside
C. primitive
D. sweet

51. The prefix cata- means:

A. down
B. conduction
C. childbirth
D. lateral

52. The prefix di- means:

A. dimension
B. distance
C. two
D. ten

53. The prefix extra- means:

A. large
B. outside
C. big
D. fast

54. The prefix per- means:

A. pressure
B. primitive
C. same
D. through

55. The prefix pachy- means:

A. thick
B. life
C. fat
D. sharp

56. The prefix pleio- means:

A. itching
B. to grow
C. more
D. upon

57. The prefix sarco- means:

A. without
B. muscular
C. volume
D. new

58. The prefix sub- means:

A. superior
B. above
C. again
D. under

59. The prefix ex- means:

A. away from
B. anus
C. bone
D. difficult

60. The prefix dia- means:

A. diameter
B. itching
C. darkness
D. through

Chapter 3 - Round 4 Correct Answer Sheet

46. D

47. C

48. A

49. B

50. D

51. A

52. C

53. B

54. D

55. A

56. C

57. B

58. D

59. A

60. D

Chapter 4 - True or False

Chapter 4 - Round 1 Questions

1. The prefix ab- means away from

A. True
B. False

2. The prefix apo- means itching

A. True
B. False

3. The prefix brady- means outside

A. True
B. False

4. The prefix clostr- means spindle

A. True
B. False

5. The prefix de- means from

A. True
B. False

6. The prefix dif- means small

A. True
B. False

7. The prefix ec- means away

A. True
B. False

8. The prefix gluco- means sweet

A. True
B. False

9. The prefix sarco- means equal

A. True
B. False

10. The prefix onco- means volume

A. True
B. False

11. The prefix parvo- means strength

A. True
B. False

12. The prefix post- means after

A. True
B. False

13. The prefix retro- means primitive

A. True
B. False

14. The prefix sub- means under

A. True
B. False

15. The prefix trans- means toward

A. True
B. False

Chapter 4 - Round 1 Correct Answer Sheet

1. A

2. B

3. B

4. A

5. A

6. B

7. A

8. A

9. B

10. A

11. B

12. A

13. B

14. A

15. B

Chapter 4 - Round 2 Questions

16. The prefix ad- means new

A. True
B. False

17. The prefix arch- means primitive

A. True
B. False

18. The prefix cis- means sweet

A. True
B. False

19. The prefix cycl- means cycle

A. True
B. False

20. The prefix dromo- means bone

A. True
B. False

21. The prefix extra- means outside

A. True
B. False

22. The prefix infra- means below

A. True
B. False

23. The prefix karyo- means fast

A. True
B. False

24. The prefix myri- means thousand

A. True
B. False

25. The prefix para- means abnormal

A. True
B. False

26. The prefix pleio- means pressure

A. True
B. False

27. The prefix oxy- means thick

A. True
B. False

28. The prefix scoto- means darkness

A. True
B. False

29. The prefix tachy- means fast

A. True
B. False

30. The prefix toco- means childbirth

A. True
B. False

Chapter 4 - Round 2 Correct Answer Sheet

16. B

17. A

18. B

19. A

20. B

21. A

22. A

23. B

24. B

25. A

26. B

27. B

28. A

29. A

30. A

Chapter 4 - Round 3 Questions

31. The prefix an- means away from

A. True
B. False

32. The prefix bi- means double

A. True
B. False

33. The prefix com- means emotions

A. True
B. False

34. The prefix dys- means difficult

A. True
B. False

35. The prefix fore- means ahead

A. True
B. False

36. The prefix iso- means life

A. True
B. False

37. The prefix normo- means few

A. True
B. False

38. The prefix per- means through

A. True
B. False

39. The prefix re- means backward

A. True
B. False

40. The prefix sito- means food

A. True
B. False

41. The prefix therap- means tense

A. True
B. False

42. The prefix ultra- means before

A. True
B. False

43. The prefix neo- means new

A. True
B. False

44. The prefix pauci- means separation

A. True
B. False

45. The prefix prim- means first

A. True
B. False

Chapter 4 - Round 3 Correct Answer Sheet

31. B

32. A

33. B

34. A

35. A

36. B

37. B

38. A

39. A

40. A

41. B

42. B

43. A

44. B

45. A

Chapter 4 - Round 4 Questions

46. The prefix ana- means after

A. True
B. False

47. The prefix bio- means life

A. True
B. False

48. The prefix cata- means down

A. True
B. False

49. The prefix cutane- means conduction

A. True
B. False

50. The prefix di- means two

A. True
B. False

51. The prefix dia- means through

A. True
B. False

52. The prefix eu- means from

A. True
B. False

53. The prefix hyper- means beyond normal

A. True
B. False

54. The prefix milli- means ten thousandth

A. True
B. False

55. The prefix ossi- means bone

A. True
B. False

56. The prefix phyt- means to on this side

A. True
B. False

57. The prefix pre- means before

A. True
B. False

58. The prefix semi- means one-half

A. True
B. False

59. The prefix super- means big

A. True
B. False

60. The prefix tetan- means tense

A. True
B. False

Chapter 4 - Round 4 Correct Answer Sheet

46. B

47. A

48. A

49. B

50. A

51. A

52. B

53. A

54. B

55. A

56. B

57. A

58. A

59. B

60. A

Answer Form

Chapter 1 - What does the prefix refer to?

Round 1 Questions

1. A B C D
2. A B C D
3. A B C D
4. A B C D
5. A B C D
6. A B C D
7. A B C D
8. A B C D
9. A B C D
10. A B C D
11. A B C D
12. A B C D
13. A B C D
14. A B C D
15. A B C D

Round 2 Questions

16. A B C D
17. A B C D
18. A B C D
19. A B C D
20. A B C D
21. A B C D
22. A B C D
23. A B C D
24. A B C D
25. A B C D
26. A B C D
27. A B C D
28. A B C D
29. A B C D
30. A B C D

Round 3 Questions

31.	A	B	C	D
32.	A	B	C	D
33.	A	B	C	D
34.	A	B	C	D
35.	A	B	C	D
36.	A	B	C	D
37.	A	B	C	D
38.	A	B	C	D
39.	A	B	C	D
40.	A	B	C	D
41.	A	B	C	D
42.	A	B	C	D
43.	A	B	C	D
44.	A	B	C	D
45.	A	B	C	D

Round 4 Questions

46.	A	B	C	D
47.	A	B	C	D
48.	A	B	C	D
49.	A	B	C	D
50.	A	B	C	D
51.	A	B	C	D
52.	A	B	C	D
53.	A	B	C	D
54.	A	B	C	D
55.	A	B	C	D
56.	A	B	C	D
57.	A	B	C	D
58.	A	B	C	D
59.	A	B	C	D
60.	A	B	C	D

Chapter 2 - Recognize the meaning of the prefix

Round 1 Questions

1.	A	B	C	D
2.	A	B	C	D
3.	A	B	C	D
4.	A	B	C	D
5.	A	B	C	D
6.	A	B	C	D
7.	A	B	C	D
8.	A	B	C	D
9.	A	B	C	D
10.	A	B	C	D
11.	A	B	C	D
12.	A	B	C	D
13.	A	B	C	D
14.	A	B	C	D
15.	A	B	C	D

Round 2 Questions

16.	A	B	C	D
17.	A	B	C	D
18.	A	B	C	D
19.	A	B	C	D
20.	A	B	C	D
21.	A	B	C	D
22.	A	B	C	D
23.	A	B	C	D
24.	A	B	C	D
25.	A	B	C	D
26.	A	B	C	D
27.	A	B	C	D
28.	A	B	C	D
29.	A	B	C	D
30.	A	B	C	D

Round 3 Questions

31.	A	B	C	D
32.	A	B	C	D
33.	A	B	C	D
34.	A	B	C	D
35.	A	B	C	D
36.	A	B	C	D
37.	A	B	C	D
38.	A	B	C	D
39.	A	B	C	D
40.	A	B	C	D
41.	A	B	C	D
42.	A	B	C	D
43.	A	B	C	D
44.	A	B	C	D
45.	A	B	C	D

Round 4 Questions

46.	A	B	C	D
47.	A	B	C	D
48.	A	B	C	D
49.	A	B	C	D
50.	A	B	C	D
51.	A	B	C	D
52.	A	B	C	D
53.	A	B	C	D
54.	A	B	C	D
55.	A	B	C	D
56.	A	B	C	D
57.	A	B	C	D
58.	A	B	C	D
59.	A	B	C	D
60.	A	B	C	D

Chapter 3 - What does the prefix mean?

Round 1 Questions

1.	A	B	C	D
2.	A	B	C	D
3.	A	B	C	D
4.	A	B	C	D
5.	A	B	C	D
6.	A	B	C	D
7.	A	B	C	D
8.	A	B	C	D
9.	A	B	C	D
10.	A	B	C	D
11.	A	B	C	D
12.	A	B	C	D
13.	A	B	C	D
14.	A	B	C	D
15.	A	B	C	D

Round 2 Questions

16.	A	B	C	D
17.	A	B	C	D
18.	A	B	C	D
19.	A	B	C	D
20.	A	B	C	D
21.	A	B	C	D
22.	A	B	C	D
23.	A	B	C	D
24.	A	B	C	D
25.	A	B	C	D
26.	A	B	C	D
27.	A	B	C	D
28.	A	B	C	D
29.	A	B	C	D
30.	A	B	C	D

Round 3 Questions

31.	A	B	C	D
32.	A	B	C	D
33.	A	B	C	D
34.	A	B	C	D
35.	A	B	C	D
36.	A	B	C	D
37.	A	B	C	D
38.	A	B	C	D
39.	A	B	C	D
40.	A	B	C	D
41.	A	B	C	D
42.	A	B	C	D
43.	A	B	C	D
44.	A	B	C	D
45.	A	B	C	D

Round 4 Questions

46.	A	B	C	D
47.	A	B	C	D
48.	A	B	C	D
49.	A	B	C	D
50.	A	B	C	D
51.	A	B	C	D
52.	A	B	C	D
53.	A	B	C	D
54.	A	B	C	D
55.	A	B	C	D
56.	A	B	C	D
57.	A	B	C	D
58.	A	B	C	D
59.	A	B	C	D
60.	A	B	C	D

Chapter 4 - True or False

Round 1 Questions

1.	A	B
2.	A	B
3.	A	B
4.	A	B
5.	A	B
6.	A	B
7.	A	B
8.	A	B
9.	A	B
10.	A	B
11.	A	B
12.	A	B
13.	A	B
14.	A	B
15.	A	B

Round 2 Questions

16.	A	B
17.	A	B
18.	A	B
19.	A	B
20.	A	B
21.	A	B
22.	A	B
23.	A	B
24.	A	B
25.	A	B
26.	A	B
27.	A	B
28.	A	B
29.	A	B
30.	A	B

Round 3 Questions

31.	A	B
32.	A	B
33.	A	B
34.	A	B
35.	A	B
36.	A	B
37.	A	B
38.	A	B
39.	A	B
40.	A	B
41.	A	B
42.	A	B
43.	A	B
44.	A	B
45.	A	B

Round 4 Questions

46.	A	B
47.	A	B
48.	A	B
49.	A	B
50.	A	B
51.	A	B
52.	A	B
53.	A	B
54.	A	B
55.	A	B
56.	A	B
57.	A	B
58.	A	B
59.	A	B
60.	A	B

Final Words

I hope you enjoyed reading this quiz book as much as I enjoyed making it. It was truly a labor of love.

I'm always striving to improve my books, and one of the ways I can do that is if I get an honest feedback on my work.

It would help me out a lot if you could leave your honest review.

Thank you so much for doing this!

Alexander McRose

Printed in Great Britain
by Amazon